TERESA'S ECSTASY

Begonya Plaza

BROADWAY PLAY PUBLISHING INC
224 E 62nd St, NY, NY 10065
www.broadwayplaypub.com
info@broadwayplaypub.com

TERESA'S ECSTASY
© Copyright 2013 by Begonya Plaza

First printing: May 2013
I S B N: 978-0-88145-571-7

Book design: Marie Donovan
Page make-up: Adobe Indesign
Typeface: Palatino
Printed and bound in the U S A

TERESA'S ECSTASY was first produced by Avila Productions (Executive Producer, Jack Sharkey; Producer, Jim Weiner) at the Cherry Lane Theatre opening on 14 March 2012. The cast and creative contributors were:

CARLOTTA ....Begonya Plaza
ANDRÉS...Shawn Elliott
BECKY ....Linda Larkin

Director..Will Pomerantz
Set design...Adrian W Jones
Costume design.. Suzanne Chesney
Lighting design ....Scott Clyve
Sound design.. Jane Shaw
Original music.. Albert Carbonell
Assistant set design ....Katherine Akiko Day
Stage management .... Michael Alifanz
                           & Amanda Bertie Michaels
Assistant stage management ....Matt Hundley
Production management..............................Jeffrey Toombs
Public relations .... Karen Greco
General management ....Boat Rocker Entertainment
Associate producer .... Ashley Fellman
Associate producer ....Alena Chinault

CHARACTERS & SETTING

CARLOTTA PARDO, *or Carla, late 30s. An American writer, searching.*

ANDRÉS MORENO, *or Andy, late 40s. A Catalán "artiste".*

BECKY COHEN, *30s. Jewish. An empowered magazine editior from New York.*

Present day, at the home/studio of ANDRÉS MORENO *in Barcelona.*

(A large loft area, unpretentious yet sophisticated, comfortable, and creative. Upstage center there is an easel with wheels, next to it an outdated wall phone. Buckets of paint, brushes, sculptures, and other art materials are scattered on the floor and tables. Small and large framed canvases pile against each other. Upstage right there is a hallway that leads to the entrance door, and continues on to other back rooms. Stage right there is a bookshelf, filled with books, between two large windows ceiling high, looking out to a view of the Plaza de la Virreina. There is a skylight in the center of the ceiling over a large dining room table used for working, eating or playing a game of chess. A side table holds an outdated computer, a large portable C D player, and more books stacked high. Two large speakers on each side stand on the floor. A worn out well-crafted couch divides the area. Stage left is a large window. Downstage left is a Japanese moveable divider to the tasteful kitchen area, where a small breakfast table holds a traditional leg of Jamon Iberico, fastened onto its own cutting board.)

(At rise: The sun's afternoon rays shine through the windows. It is past siesta hour. The sounds of children playing ball in the plaza down below are heard, along with an occasional motorbike zipping by. The church bells ring three o'clock. A suitcase stands in the middle of the room.)

(CARLOTTA is reviewing her flight documents and calendar book as she stands next to the phone on the wall. ANDRÉS enters from up stage left and grabs a piece of newspaper to dry the sweat from his forehead.)

CARLOTTA: *(Into phone) Si, yo soy* Carlotta Pardo...*de Nueva York....Nada? No puede ser..Supervisor por favor. (She covers the mouthpiece.)* Great, now they're gonna have me on hold forever.

(ANDRÉS moves the suitcase from the center of the room to the side, out of the way.)

ANDRÉS: *La ostia, que calor!*

CARLOTTA: *Hola?* Supervisor?

(ANDRÉS crosses to kitchen, opens a refrigerator door, takes out a bottle of cold mineral "Vichy Catalán Water", cuts a few pieces of lemon, grabs two glasses and returns to living area.)

CARLOTTA: You speak English, great. Listen, my friend and I took last night's flight from J F K, same plane, same check-in time, and her luggage arrived but mine didn't? ...Really? *(To ANDRÉS)* that happens a lot... *(back to phone)* I don't think so, because you see my suitcase was on the luggage belt next to my friend's suitcase, both heading to the same plane, I saw it, so you guys here have to have it.

(ANDRÉS takes a newspaper and wipes the sweat from his forehead.)

ANDRÉS: *Tranquilizate mi amor.*

CARLOTTA: ...I really don't care who's fault it is, just find my freakin' suitcase... When's the next flight? It better, I leave Barcelona tomorrow morning, and I need mi maleta... No, our return flight is out of Madrid... With all due respect, it's your job to... Hello? Hello? Hello? *(Hangs up the phone on the wall.)* He hung up on me.

ANDRÉS: *Joder,* I'd hang up on you too.

CARLOTTA: I see you haven't changed. *(She drinks.)*

ANDRÉS: You can always count on my charm and good looks.

CARLOTTA: Good water. I missed this water.

ANDRÉS: That's not all you've missed.

CARLOTTA: Oh yeah? *(Checks her calendar pad as he studies her.)*

ANDRÉS: You've changed though…

CARLOTTA: Oh yeah?

ANDRÉS: Very New York.

CARLOTTA: And depression free.

ANDRÉS: But anxiety ridden. *(He again wipes the sweat off his forehead and neck with the newspaper.)*

CARLOTTA: Aren't we all?

(CARLOTTA looks at ANDRÉS strangely.)

ANDRÉS: What's wrong? *(He continues to wipe.)*

CARLOTTA: You wipe your sweat off with a newspaper?

ANDRÉS: Yeah, so what? That's how we do it here in Spain.

CARLOTTA: I don't remember you doing that.

ANDRÉS: Because you were blinded by love.

CARLOTTA: Yeah, with your charm and good looks. How can a suitcase get lost on a direct flight? It's absurd. It better arrive tonight like they promised.

ANDRÉS: You just got here, where are you going tomorrow morning?

CARLOTTA: You know where I'm going.

ANDRÉS: Tomorrow morning?

CARLOTTA: Yes, I told you, we need to be in Avila tomorrow.

ANDRÉS: *Para que?*

CARLOTTA: *Para que?* What do you mean, *para que?*

ANDRÉS: *Para que!* You forgot Spanish?

CARLOTTA: I know what *para que* means. I just don't get why you ask *para que*.

ANDRÉS: Avila? There's nothing there.

CARLOTTA: I'm writing a story about Saint Teresa of Avila.

ANDRÉS: Oh right. That slut.

CARLOTTA: What? Why do you say that?

ANDRÉS: She had orgasms with Jesus. It's a known fact.

CARLOTTA: That's ludicrous and preposterous!

ANDRÉS: Here in Spain that's how she's known.

CARLOTTA: I'm not interested in some misconstrued interpretation of this saintly woman's transcendental love for God.

ANDRÉS: God? *(Laughs boisterously)* Don't make me laugh. *Escuchame*, there is no God! The beginning of the universe was nothing but frozen helium, which is what created what we are all now. Propelled by a bang, an explosion of cosmic proportions, life here on earth was triggered. *Y esa es la simple verdad.*

CARLOTTA: Frozen helium!

ANDRÉS: It's the truth, pure and simple.

CARLOTTA: You don't know that.

ANDRÉS: How can nuns say they're married to Jesus, and Teresa, writing love letters to a man who died thousands of years ago, *Venga ya!*

CARLOTTA: It's a metaphor!

ANDRÉS: Like indigenous peoples, I worship the laws of nature, earth, sun, moon, the stars, creation, and yes, the big bang! *"Ese accidente de energia cosmica…"*

CARLOTTA: Andy! *(Pause)* Does Becky have a clean towel?

(CARLOTTA tries to go out to other room, but ANDRÉS stops her.)

ANDRÉS: Claro, all my towels are clean. Mira, that literal God humanized by most people, Carla, does not exist. That Catholic God who sends his son to earth to battle the sins of the world is *una buenisima historia,* and religions design those heroic tales of inexplicable beings, to spark the imagination in order to manipulate the people—

(BECKY appears, wearing a travel robe, barefoot with a towel on her head.)

BECKY: He's got a point.

ANDRÉS: Sensible woman.

BECKY: I personally believe that religion needs to accept science and the natural progression of our times, otherwise we're just gonna continue not giving a shit.

(Beat)

ANDRÉS: Where are you from Becky?

BECKY: Philly. For me everything is mathematical. It all mysteriously adds up in the end.

ANDRÉS: How was your shower? Did you find everything you needed?

BECKY: Yeah, thanks. Do you have something cold to drink?

ANDRÉS: Of course, I have coke, water, beer, soda, fruit juice…

BECKY: What are you drinking, Carla?

CARLOTTA: Vichy Catalán. There's a spring nearby. It's salty.

BECKY: I like salty.

(BECKY *reaches for* CARLOTTA'*s glass.*)

CARLOTTA: And so good for you too. I love this water.

(BECKY *tastes the water.*)

BECKY: Ewww.

(BECKY *hands the water back to* CARLOTTA.)

ANDRÉS: I also have a nice white wine.

BECKY: Wine at this hour?

ANDRÉS: I didn't know there was an appropriate hour for wine drinking.

BECKY: Usually alcoholic drinks are reserved for "happy hour".

ANDRÉS: Really? How confining.

BECKY: No. Just responsible.

ANDRÉS: Or repressive.

(CARLOTTA *holds up her glass.*)

CARLOTTA: This water's got medicinal properties. It cures the sick.

BECKY: I'm not sick. *(She looks at her cell phone.)* Shit, my battery's dead, "Andrés," *(Over enunciating the "r")* do you mind passing me that phone?

ANDRÉS: That phone? *(Points)*

BECKY: Yeah that phone right there, do you mind?

ANDRÉS: No I don't mind, only it's attached to the wall. *(He lifts the phone off the receiver.)*

BECKY: You're joking.

ANDRÉS: No.

BECKY: Do you have a cell phone?

ANDRÉS: No.

BECKY: I can't believe this.

CARLOTTA: He's kidding.

ANDRÉS: I've got another phone in my bedroom. If you want some privacy I'll gladly show you to it.

BECKY: I know where your bedroom is. I'll take a Coke if you don't mind.

(ANDRÉS *crosses to the kitchen.*)

BECKY: My stomach's feeling a little queasy, how's yours, Carla?

CARLOTTA: Except for my suitcase, I'm just fine.

BECKY: Did you call the airline?

CARLOTTA: Yeah, they said it should arrive tonight.

BECKY: Good. So get yourself ready and let's go out!

CARLOTTA: I can't. Not right now.

BECKY: Paco's got the night planned out for us.

CARLOTTA: Go without me, Beck.

BECKY: We're only here for one night…

ANDRÉS: Precisely.

BECKY: *(To* ANDRÉS*)* I want Carla to meet Paco, my business associate, who lives here in Barcelona, and knows everyone worth knowing.

(ANDRÉS *hands* BECKY *the can of Coke.*)

BECKY: He swears we haven't seen anything like the Barcelona night life.

ANDRÉS: What is it you do exactly, Becky?

CARLOTTA: I told you, Becky's the editor of a magazine called, Beyond Reason, for which I'm writing the story about Saint Teresa.

ANDRÉS: *(To* BECKY*)* You find Teresa of Avila interesting?

BECKY: Why not? A brilliant Jewish feminist during the Spanish Inquisition, are you kidding me? Why wouldn't I find Saint Teresa interesting, and especially with Carla writing about her?

CARLOTTA: High expectations, the pressure's on!

ANDRÉS: What religion are you, Becky?

BECKY: I'm not religious. Just proud to be born Jewish.

ANDRÉS: Santa Teresa was a Catholic...

BECKY: But of Jewish blood. An associate of mine gave me a collection of Carla's writing, and that night I read all of it, couldn't put it down, wondering how I could never have heard about her. The very next morning I get a phone call from Carlotta Pardo, proposing to me, this story!

CARLOTTA: And so here we are.

ANDRÉS: *Que bien.* Lucky me.

(BECKY *studies a small painting on the wall.)*

BECKY: I like this painting. A little larger maybe with a little more yellow in the background. It would go perfect in my hallway where the wall is pastel blue.

ANDRÉS: A match made in heaven.

BECKY: How much?

ANDRÉS: Oh, I don't know...five thousand.

BECKY: I'll send you a check.

ANDRÉS: Cash only, sorry. And Euros.

BECKY: What's wrong with Dollars? *(Beat)* Fine, that's, but then you will have to put a little more yellow in the background.

ANDRÉS: That I won't do. Sorry. Change your wall color.

(BECKY *hands* ANDRÉS *the empty can of Coke.*)

BECKY: Oh well. Excuse me.

ANDRÉS: Be my guest.

(ANDRÉS *crumples the can as* BECKY *exits to bedroom.*)

ANDRÉS: *Que mierda de mujer!*

CARLOTTA: For wanting to buy your painting?

ANDRÉS: That air of entitlement! No manners, so American! I should have asked her for ten thousand!

CARLOTTA: You seemed to like her very much at first.

ANDRÉS: She's disrespectful, Carlotta.

CARLOTTA: No, she's not.

ANDRÉS: Does she know about me? What did you tell her?

CARLOTTA: Nothing really. I don't know… that you're a good friend who I was married to long ago..

ANDRÉS: I'm your husband, Carlotta. Long ago? Only two years ago I was with you in New York.

CARLOTTA: Say no more…

ANDRÉS: You like it this way.

CARLOTTA: I'm liking it so much, that I even brought the divorce papers with me.

(Beat)

ANDRÉS: Who encouraged you to write?

CARLOTTA: You did.

ANDRÉS: The drafts and drafts of shitty writing you put me through…

CARLOTTA: And it's a good thing I didn't listen to your discouraging responses.

ANDRÉS: Just wanted the best for you. By the way, she's not making any long distance phone calls I hope.

CARLOTTA: She's calling her partner here in Barcelona.

ANDRÉS: Because she seems the typical chick with money, entitled, presuming she knows more than anyone else. Telling me how to paint? To add more yellow to my canvas? What is she, crazy? I'm not selling her *mierda*! *(He lights a cigarette.)*

CARLOTTA: That's dumb, you could use the money.

ANDRÉS: It's not always about money, Carlotta.

CARLOTTA: Still smoking, huh?

ANDRÉS: Still smoking. *(Pause)* You know, Carlotta, what matters to me are good sentiments, empathy, "synergy"…

CARLOTTA: Where was all that when we were married?

ANDRÉS: We're still married.

(ANDRÉS passes the cigarette and CARLOTTA puts it out in the ashtray.)

CARLOTTA: On paper.

ANDRÉS: I gave you wings to fly as high as …

CARLOTTA: Oh, is that how you see it?

ANDRÉS: You think that was easy?

CARLOTTA: Much easier than a day-to-day commitment.

(BECKY enters, dressed in jeans, silk flowery blouse, no bra, high heeled sandals. An expensive watch, diamond earrings, make-up case.)

BECKY: "Andrrrésss," thank you for being so kind and allowing me to use your phone.

ANDRÉS: Don't mention it, and call me Andy—it's a lot less effort.

(BECKY *stuffs clothes and make-up into her suitcase. Grabs a tube of body cream and a nail file.*)

BECKY: So, you coming, Carla?

CARLOTTA: Becky, I really want to, but I can't.

BECKY: Andy's welcome to join us if he likes, I guess.

ANDRÉS: Sorry, we want to spend a little time together. Alone.

(ANDRÉS *lovingly puts his hands on* CARLOTTA'*s shoulders.* BECKY *rubs body cream on her arms.*)

BECKY: *(Laughs)* Okay, I understand. How about I stay at Paco's tonight then and give you a little more time alone?

ANDRÉS: *Que buena* idea.

(CARLOTTA *takes* ANDRÉS' *hands off her.*)

CARLOTTA: Beck, you come back here tonight.

BECKY: Nah, besides it'll get late, I'll be wasted. Lets just meet at the train station tomorrow.

ANDRÉS: Yeah Carlotta, it's much easier for her that way.

CARLOTTA: But you don't have to stay at Paco's, you know that.

(BECKY *grabs a nail file.*)

BECKY: It'll be good to spend some time with him, and his home is spectacular. Up on this mountain called Tibidabo, with views of Barcelona. When I interviewed him for the job he insisted it be at his home over a lunch that he'd prepare himself. *(Laughs)* The presentation alone won me over. He runs the Spain office for me here, and he's terrific. I think he wants me to meet his new boyfriend tonight, who he says is "un bombón." The last one he had was a terror, and awful how he made poor Paco cry. Imagine long distance, hearing him wailing over the phone, complaining about his cheating partner, with an accent. But because I sensed he had potential, I gave him a little time. Some people deserve a chance. I knew that once he "got it," you know, understood that he had to get rid of that loser and stop playing the victim, he'd be fine.

ANDRÉS: *Fantastica…*

BECKY: And now he's got Barcelona's "elite" in the palm of his hand. That's how good he is, and business is booming. I hope this new boyfriend deserves him. I wish you could meet him, Carla.

CARLOTTA: Next time.

BECKY: We're gonna have to come back again.

(CARLOTTA *shies from responding.*)

BECKY: Do you like this top?

CARLOTTA: Yeah, very much…

(BECKY *looks to* ANDRÉS.)

ANDRÉS: Not so much.

BECKY: No? Why?

ANDRÉS: Something about it… (*He walks over to* BECKY *touches the silk colorful fabric. His hand slides down her back.*) Too much… yellow.

BECKY: Really? Where's the mirror?

ANDRÉS: Bathroom.

BECKY: Not the one above the sink?

ANDRÉS: *Si, claro.*

BECKY: You don't have a full length one?

(ANDRÉS *points to her suitcase.*)

ANDRÉS: What else you got in there?

(BECKY *pulls a T-shirt out from the open suitcase. She shows shirt to* ANDRÉS. CARLOTTA, *who has wandered over to the bookcase, finds her old journal on shelf.*)

ANDRÉS: Try it on.

(BECKY *thinks about it and starts to walk away.*)

ANDRÉS: No, no, *aquí.*

BECKY: Thank you very much, but I think I'll change in the bathroom.

(ANDRÉS *grabs his drawing pad.*)

ANDRÉS: Tonta, don't be shy.

BECKY: I don't have a bra on…

(ANDRÉS *sketches* BECKY *with a flair. She likes the attention.*)

ANDRÉS: So?

BECKY: I'm not undressing in front of you.

ANDRÉS: Afraid of showing me your little titties?

BECKY: I'm not afraid of anything.

ANDRÉS: Then stay still and don't move. (*He begins to sketch.*)

BECKY: That's okay, but I'm not undressing in front of you.

ANDRÉS: (*Flamboyantly*) An "artist" has no gender nor judgment. Come on, off with the top.

BECKY: (*Laughs*) I won't give you the pleasure.

ANDRÉS: On the contrary, the pleasure is all yours.

CARLOTTA: Andy!

ANDRÉS: Look, Carlotta, *sus pezones se han puesto durísimos.* Your hard nipples are as they say in America, "a dead giveaway".

BECKY: Keep on wishing.

(BECKY *grabs shirts and exits.* ANDRÉS *laughs.*)

CARLOTTA: What's gotten into you? "An artist has no gender nor judgment?"

ANDRÉS: This is one man she does not intimidate.

CARLOTTA: So that's what it's about?

ANDRÉS: Please. Uptight over a pair of tits—just go out here to the beach and you'll see millions of them, all ages, shapes and sizes. Remember the series I did of your voluptuous breasts?

CARLOTTA: Yes, and I want those back by the way.

ANDRÉS: You didn't like them. You said, they didn't look like yours.

CARLOTTA: That's true.

ANDRÉS: She's full of herself. She lacks *"sentido comun"*.

CARLOTTA: You just met her.

ANDRÉS: Exactly, and look at the impression she's already left on me.

CARLOTTA: Your problema, no one else's.

ANDRÉS: My only problema, is that you haven't given me a hug yet.

(CARLOTTA *is touched seeing* ANDRÉS *with open arms.*)

CARLOTTA: I haven't? You're right. The suitcase threw me off.

(BECKY *enters with hair up, gelled. Wears a new top with the tags still on.*)

BECKY: I need scissors.

(BECKY *looks around, opens a drawer.* ANDRÉS *is distracted. He looks at* CARLOTTA, *then back to* BECKY.)

BECKY: Don't mind me, I'll find something…I'm sure.

(ANDRÉS *and* CARLOTTA *begin to hug.* BECKY *pulls
out a switchblade and easily pops it open as she stares at
them hugging. She walks over to them carrying the open
switchblade.* ANDRÉS *steps back at the sight.*)

BECKY: Sorry, Carla, do you mind?

(BECKY *shows the tags on the back of her new blouse.*
CARLOTTA *takes the knife and cuts the tags off.*)

BECKY: Thanks. Go back to your hug. Oh, let me take a
picture?

(ANDRÉS *and* CARLOTTA *embrace again.* BECKY *takes a
picture with her i-phone.*)

BECKY: For old times' sake.

ANDRÉS: *Que coñazo de mujer!*

BECKY: What does that mean? (*She stares at him.*)

ANDRÉS: That…you're a pleasure to be with.

BECKY: Thank you. You know, we were wondering if
you'd be interested in illustrating Carla's story for the
magazine.

ANDRÉS: Oh I don't know about that. First lets see what
Carlotta writes.

CARLOTTA: You would have to paint images of an
"inexplicable being", but in human form, perfect and
eternal…

ANDRÉS: No, no, no, no, what if they were abstract
images? Say…of star dust? (*Exhilarated*)

(*From a chaotic explosion of hot energy, whirling, weaving,
squeezing, exploding, the insides pulsing into this balancing
act of cosmic matter…*)

CARLOTTA: And Teresa holding the hand of God in the
center of it all!

ANDRÉS: That is out of the question!

BECKY: You're so dogmatic.

ANDRÉS: Me? Not me. It's the church that's dogmatic with its outdated, rigid views! What I see are subatomic particles traveling in space, dancing around, who knows when and where.

BECKY: Well, after Avila, Carla will have a better idea of what she wants.

CARLOTTA: Yeah, lets not get ahead of ourselves...

ANDRÉS: I can tell you right now without a doubt, I will not illustrate a "God" in our own image. That's not what I do.

BECKY: Excuse me, I think I left my lipstick in the bathroom. *(She exits.)*

CARLOTTA: You could have said thank you. It would be nice working together even while we're getting a divorce.

ANDRÉS: Divorce? What divorce?

CARLOTTA: The one we've been putting off for the past few years.

(Pause)

ANDRÉS: You're kidding.

CARLOTTA: The papers are in my suitcase.

ANDRÉS: That doesn't do us much good.

CARLOTTA: They'll be here. You'll see.

ANDRÉS: All I see is that you turn me on every time.

CARLOTTA: That's not enough.

ANDRÉS: I meant to tell you, religious institutions were the first corporations...

CARLOTTA: What does that have to do with my dear, Saint Teresa.

ANDRÉS: Well, that she spearheaded a religious order as part of the Catholic Church, which preaches compassion and love while turning a blind eye to warmongers.

CARLOTTA: I keep telling you, I'm not interested in religion per se. I'm interested in Teresa and her message. Her example.

ANDRÉS: She was part of an institution that excludes, kills, exploits and brainwashes people…

CARLOTTA: Teresa overcame all of that! While living with death threatening illnesses, defamations, ethnic and religious genocide by the Spanish Inquisition! She reformed her own church, founded over a dozen monasteries, all the while writing masterworks of literature. For her, these challenges proved that the trials we endure are nothing compared to the battle we have inside when practicing quiet, mental prayer, mysticism, which she affirms is the ultimate act of love. Love is God

ANDRÉS: But God is an invention to control the masses for power, and wealth, that's all I'm saying.

CARLOTTA: Stop blaming others and start looking inside yourself, that's all Teresa is saying.

ANDRÉS: *(Playfully)* I'm just an artist who questions and probes.

CARLOTTA: Then do it.

(BECKY enters wearing a new top, holding her pink lipstick and other clothes.)

BECKY: That's it, I'm not changing anymore.

ANDRÉS: The other shirt fit you better, Becky.

CARLOTTA: You look great, don't listen to him.

BECKY: I can't picture the two of you married.

ANDRÉS: I can't picture it any other way.

BECKY: They do say opposites attract. How about that glass of white wine now? It's getting to be that hour, somewhere.

ANDRÉS: Happy hour! Finally! (*He crosses to the kitchen, pulls a bottle of white wine from the fridge and uncorks it.*)

CARLOTTA: I really do wish I was going with you...

BECKY: They'll be more opportunities . Go to bed early, get some rest for us both.

(*Pours three glasses.*)

CARLOTTA: I know, tomorrow's morning meeting is followed by three hours of prayer.

BECKY: That's great! I've never done something like that.

CARLOTTA: Me neither.

(ANDRÉS *gives each woman a glass.*)

ANDRÉS: Don't worry, five minutes and the novelty will have worn off.

BECKY: Tonight I'm meeting Catalán aristocracy, according to Paco.

ANDRÉS: Here's to aristocracy, bureaucracy, and oligarchy! *Salud!*

(*They clink.*)

BECKY: How about instead, to,Teresa!

CARLOTTA: Yes, to, Teresa!

ANDRÉS: Teresa, another victim of her culture. Did you know that the Catholic Church pardoned anybody's most abhorring sin, for a price of earthly gold?

CARLOTTA: Andy, give it a rest already?

ANDRÉS: Should redemption of anyone's soul be a purchased commodity? That's all I'm asking.

CARLOTTA: *(To* BECKY*)* He doesn't get that life has a price.

ANDRÉS: Nor do I seem to get that her famous ecstasies were sexual orgasms. How did she get away with claiming that her expressive genitals were undergoing a spiritual, earth-shattering experience.

BECKY: Because sex and spirituality can be all in one.

CARLOTTA: Explain that to him, Beck.

BECKY: Andrés, in both instances we're letting go of our ego.

CARLOTTA: That's true-love communion…

*(*ANDRÉS *inserts a C D of Cat Stevens'. A Wild World begins to play.)*

ANDRÉS: *No se yo*, we men are way simpler than that.

BECKY: How so?

ANDRÉS: We either get a hard-on or we don't.

CARLOTTA: How evolved.

*(*ANDRÉS *starts to dance. He sings to* CARLOTTA *and pulls her to him.)*

ANDRÉS: "Oh baby, baby it's a wild world. It's hard to get by just upon a smile. Oh baby, baby it's a wild world, and I'll always remember you like a child, girl." I had this C D forever thinking he was Nina Simone. Doesn't he sound to you like Nina Simone?

BECKY: Nina Simone?

CARLOTTA: He doesn't sound like Nina Simone.

(All three listen in silence as CARLOTTA *breaks away, slowly moving to the music.* BECKY *joins.)*

ANDRÉS, BECKY & CARLOTTA: "Oh baby, baby it's a wild world and it's hard to get by just upon a smile…

oh baby, baby it's a wild world and I'll always remember you like a child, girl..."

(The three clink glasses and dance.)

CARLOTTA: Wow, I just had this flashback of my parent's home in Berkeley. My neighborhood, expansive...

ANDRÉS: The Vietnam war...

CARLOTTA: Clean, everyone happy, everything nice...

ANDRÉS: Martin Luther King's murder...

CARLOTTA: People would smile and say hello on the streets...

ANDRÉS: Robert Kennedy, and John F Kennedy, murdered...

CARLOTTA: People had hope, and doors were never locked.

ANDRÉS: The distorted memories of an innocent child.

BECKY: It was less populated and cleaner.

ANDRÉS: "Oh baby, baby it's a wild world..."

(BECKY pours herself more wine.)

BECKY: "And I'll always remember you like a child, girl..." *(To CARLOTTA)* So how did you learn Spanish growing up in Berkeley?

(ANDRÉS turns off the music.)

CARLOTTA: In College. Then came here to do my study abroad year, and stayed to finish my masters while working as a model.

BECKY: You were a model?

ANDRÉS: She had my entire art class drooling, to the point I couldn't even succumb, that unattainable luscious, naked body...

BECKY: You were a nude model?

CARLOTTA: It was a great gig. I didn't have to speak a word.

BECKY: Very provocative.

ANDRÉS: Yeah, and chaotic. I lost my teaching job.

BECKY: The price you paid…

ANDRÉS: Marriage was the price if I wanted to have sex with her.

CARLOTTA: If chaos is the organic expression of the divine, out of which all is created, then I expect only good ultimately.

BECKY: Yes, go Teresa!

(BECKY *and* CARLOTTA *clink glasses.*)

ANDRÉS: Teresa, the crackpot. She was addicted to *opio*, you know…

CARLOTTA: Andy, what ever…

ANDRÉS: *Sabes, opio, es una droga euforica?*

CARLOTTA: I know, euphoric…

ANDRÉS: So she wasn't seeing God, she was hallucinating. *(Lights a cigarette)*

BECKY: Why couldn't she be doing both?

CARLOTTA: He's trying to defame, Teresa.

ANDRÉS: Opium was the common prescriptive drug during her time. Just like, Samuel Taylor Coleridge, who wrote poems inspired by opium-induced dreams. "In Xanadu did Kubla Khan a stately pleasure-dome decree. Where Alph the sacred river ran, through caverns measureless to man, down to a sunless sea…" *(Tries to remember more, but can't. Angry)* I used to know it all, but possibly hash has been clouding my perceptions.

CARLOTTA: You ingested that much?

ANDRÉS: I can't remember.

BECKY: You have to put this in your story, Carla.

CARLOTTA: Do I?

BECKY: If that was the prescriptive drug…

CARLOTTA: No. Teresa was not on opium!

ANDRÉS: The ecstasy of Saint Teresa was prophetic intoxication! Don't you find it more interesting seeing how she played the church in order to not be condemned as a heretic. The woman was brilliant.

CARLOTTA: You're provoking with your vulgarizations.

BECKY: Carla, I take it back. You write your story any way you want to.

ANDRÉS: Okay, and no more Teresa.

CARLOTTA: Isn't that what your magazine is about?

(BECKY *and* CARLOTTA *look at each other. Pause)*

ANDRÉS: Anyone know why Cat Steven stopped singing?

CARLOTTA: Did he stop singing?

ANDRÉS: Yeah, to become a Muslim.

CARLOTTA: That's it, I'm going with Becky. *(She stands.)*

BECKY: This, I'm afraid, is true, Carla.

CARLOTTA: Really?

ANDRÉS: Another perfect example of religion's dirty work.

CARLOTTA: How?

ANDRÉS: Twenty something years ago, Cat Stevens became Yusuf Islam, and had to obey a whole new set of rules, like stop making music and stop creating his art, his genius!

CARLOTTA: That's terrible.

(BECKY *downs her wine.*)

ANDRÉS: Creativity is the closest thing to God!!!

BECKY: I read somewhere he gave up music for terrorism.

CARLOTTA: What?

ANDRÉS: *¿Hay Dios mio, que estupideces dices?*

(BECKY *takes her suitcase.*)

BECKY: It's in the papers.

ANDRÉS: *Esta mujer está loca.*

BECKY: You are *loco*. Read the news. (*She looks at her watch.*)

Gotta go. Where's café Cuba Libre?

ANDRÉS: Around the corner, one block to your right.

BECKY: Carla, *hasta mañana.*

(BECKY *kisses* CARLOTTA *on the cheek tenderly.*)

CARLOTTA: Tomorrow morning, eight sharp, at the entrance to the train station.

BECKY: Right on! (*Starts to go, but turns back to* ANDRÉS) By the way, American radio stations don't play his music any more…

ANDRÉS: *Vete, vete de aqui, por Dios, no me hagas decir una barbaridad!!!*

BECKY: Why else do you think he's never been inducted into the Rock and Roll Hall of Fame?

ANDRÉS: Because you Americans are prejudiced and idiots. *¡Adios!*

CARLOTTA: Have fun.

BECKY: That's not it. We get even.

ANDRÉS: *Me estás tocando los cojones.*

BECKY: I know what *cojones* means.

ANDRÉS: Good.

BECKY: And you don't have any! (*She exits with a laugh.*)

ANDRÉS: *Fuera, le daría una patada en el culo…*

CARLOTTA: I love that woman.

ANDRÉS: What an idiot! One of the most peace-loving men you could ever meet, who wrote a song called *Peace Train*, she calls a terrorist?

CARLOTTA: It's like you calling Teresa a crackpot.

ANDRÉS: That's different.

CARLOTTA: And at first you were so smitten, checking her out.

ANDRÉS: Yeah, at first, until…

CARLOTTA: Until she stopped agreeing with you?

ANDRÉS: She's not my type, with all the sheet she puts on, the less *cachondo* I felt.

CARLOTTA: She's a lot like you.

ANDRÉS: Nothing like me.

CARLOTTA: I'm starving, Andy.

ANDRÉS: I know the perfect restaurant for us.

CARLOTTA: We can't, my suitcase.

ANDRÉS: Oh right. What do you feel like eating *mi amor*? How about my famous spaghetti carbonara?

CARLOTTA: Ummm. No, it's too hot for that, but how about a nice cold gazpacho? I haven't had that in a while.

ANDRÉS: *Vale.* How about that, *y una ensalada alcuzcuz*?

CARLOTTA: I'm fine just with the gazpacho.

(ANDRÉS *crosses to the kitchen, goes to the refrigerator, puts the opened wine bottle inside. Takes out a new bottle and starts opening it.* CARLOTTA *follows him.*)

CARLOTTA: Can I help?

ANDRÉS: No, you relax. I have this special wine, for us. *(Holds it up, and begins to uncork it.)* You'll see, smoother, a little drier. Goes down like water…

CARLOTTA: Wine at this hour? *(She laughs as she uncovers a leg of ham.)*

ANDRÉS: Did you see how she couldn't restrain herself from drinking like a fiend? Without any appreciation for the exquisite taste of savoring the wine.

CARLOTTA: You're sounding very conceited…

ANDRÉS: I'm not ashamed of being a *sibarita*, an epicurean, a devout hedonist.

(CARLOTTA takes a knife and cuts into the leg of ham.)

CARLOTTA: Then stop judging others.

ANDRÉS: *Cuidado* with that knife, I just got it sharpened.

CARLOTTA: I'll be okay. *(She cuts into the ham again.)*

ANDRÉS: I'll bet you anything that she won't make it to the train on time.

(CARLOTTA puts a piece in her mouth.)

CARLOTTA: Umm…soo good.

ANDRÉS: I don't have balls? She's the one running off like a scared little rabbit…

CARLOTTA: Andy, can you hold back your pejorative comments toward Becky?

ANDRÉS: *Por supuesto mi amor*, we won't discuss Santa Teresa, nor Santa Becky.

CARLOTTA: Gracias.

(CARLOTTA slowly takes another piece of ham into her mouth, as ANDRÉS watches her and serves the wine.)

CARLOTTA: Ummm, delicious. It just melts in my mouth.

ANDRÉS: Let me do it. *(He takes the knife and cuts a long, thin, beautiful slice.)* The thinner the slice, the better it tastes.

(ANDRÉS puts the slice very delicately in CARLOTTA's mouth. She closes her eyes to savor the taste.)

CARLOTTA: Ummm...*buenisimo.*

(ANDRÉS picks up the two filled glasses, and hands CARLOTTA her glass.)

ANDRÉS: *Chin chin.*

(ANDRÉS and CARLOTTA clink glasses and drink.)

CARLOTTA: Ahh. It's a good thing I don't do this everyday.

ANDRÉS: You can't get any of this in America anyway.

CARLOTTA: Nor can you get here a lot of what's in America.

ANDRÉS: Yeah, like what?

CARLOTTA: Pancake mix, peanut butter, marshmallows, barbecue... Pastrami sandwiches, stuff like that.

ANDRÉS: I miss those pancakes.

CARLOTTA: I love it here, but I love it there, too.

ANDRÉS: Where, there?

CARLOTTA: America.

ANDRÉS: America is racist, righteous, and right wing...

CARLOTTA: Europe isn't? *(She drinks.)*

ANDRÉS: New York's all unto itself, it's not America.

(CARLOTTA notices the label on the wine bottle.)

CARLOTTA: Yeah, like Barcelona isn't Spain?

ANDRÉS: Touché.

CARLOTTA: Your design?

(ANDRÉS *pulls out from the fridge: tomatoes, one green bell pepper, a red bell pepper, an onion, garlic, cucumber, olive oil, vinegar, salt and a bottle of cold water.*)

ANDRÉS: Yeah. I spent a week at their wineries. It was beautiful, and when I came home, a couple cases of wine and one of olive oil were waiting for me at my door.

CARLOTTA: I like it. You should do more of this kind of work.

(ANDRÉS *pulls out bottle of olive oil.* CARLOTTA *takes the baguette sitting on counter.*)

ANDRÉS: I'm an artist, Carlotta, not a label designer.

CARLOTTA: But you're so good at it, and it pays well, right?

ANDRÉS: This was a favor to a friend, whose team of ego-maniacs drove me insane with their endless changes and corrections, only to end up with my first label. It's just not worth the money.

(ANDRÉS *pours the olive oil into an artisan bowl.* CARLOTTA *cuts bread.*)

ANDRÉS: Some people can't sleep if they don't have money in the bank for a rainy day, but what's the point of that if it keeps them from sleeping, huh?

(CARLOTTA *dips the bread into the olive oil.*)

CARLOTTA: I like that about you…

ANDRÉS: I've missed you.

CARLOTTA: No you haven't.

ANDRÉS: It's good to have someone to talk to.

CARLOTTA: How about someone to talk with?

(ANDRÉS *prepares to chop vegetables.*)

ANDRÉS: People annoy me—women especially. I've noticed they get crazier as they get older.

CARLOTTA: And you stay sane one right?

ANDRÉS: I've never been sane. But I don't need to impress anyone, or be something I'm not. *(Pause)* Besides, I have you.

CARLOTTA: That is not true.

ANDRÉS: It's not about quantity, it's quality. Remember?

(ANDRÉS peels and chops more vegetables, masterfully and effortlessly, with gusto. CARLOTTA helps.)

CARLOTTA: We should have just stayed friends.

ANDRÉS: I was fine being friends with benefits.

CARLOTTA: Speaking of friends with benefits, how's Sandra?

ANDRÉS: Sandrita, *la que no para de hablar*? Sandrita's sweet but she doesn't get me hard. *(Considering)* Though she is loaded.

CARLOTTA: There you go. And she loves you just the way you are.

ANDRÉS: *Pero,* that shrieking laugh she lets out in the most inappropriate moments, kills me every time.

(ANDRÉS and CARLOTTA chop vegetables.)

ANDRÉS: A woman needs to be beautiful, smell good, and not say too much.

CARLOTTA: You're better off getting yourself a dog.

ANDRÉS: I've considered it, but picking up poop in public is not for me.

CARLOTTA: Sandrita loves you, what more can you ask for?

ANDRÉS: You.

(Beat)

Carlotta, you're my best friend.

CARLOTTA: And you're mine too.

ANDRÉS: Then why bring up Sandrita?

CARLOTTA: She's in your life a lot more.

ANDRÉS: It's not hurting anyone.

CARLOTTA: It's not serving anyone, but you who likes being chased by Sandrita, as the unattainable, abandoned, lonely "artiste".

(ANDRÉS takes the remote, and hits play. Cat Stevens' Father and Son *comes on.)*

ANDRÉS: Is there someone else, Carlotta?

CARLOTTA: That's not the point.

ANDRÉS: Yes it is.

CARLOTTA: Me. It's all about me now.

ANDRÉS: How self-absorbed.

CARLOTTA: Look who's talking, you don't move a finger for anyone. I'm here, and you won't even come to Avila with me.

ANDRÉS: Listen! Listen how beautifully he changes voices, the father and the son. I'm crazy about that boy. Cat Stevens is my God.

CARLOTTA: It's a shame he doesn't sing any longer.

ANDRÉS: Actually, he's singing again now.

CARLOTTA: Oh, yeah? That's great.

ANDRÉS: Except it's all about Allah. *(He goes back to dicing vegetables.)*

CARLOTTA: You heard him?

ANDRÉS: Not interested.

CARLOTTA: Why not?

(ANDRÉS *dices for the garnishes.*)

CARLOTTA: Why don't you want to hear what this God of yours sounds like now?

ANDRÉS: Anyone who buys into an organized religion loses my vote and my money.

CARLOTTA: Don't you see it's you who loses?

(Beat)

ANDRÉS: I can honestly say there's only one loss I've cared about in my life.

(Beat)

CARLOTTA: What's that?

ANDRÉS: Our child.

CARLOTTA: We weren't ready.

ANDRÉS: I wasn't ready for that.

CARLOTTA: Really? First time I hear you say that. Why didn't we ever speak?

ANDRÉS: We talked *muchisimo, siempre*, Carlotta.

CARLOTTA: About art, literature, politics, everything else under the sun, except us, never about matters of consequence.

ANDRÉS: I didn't want to make you feel worse.

CARLOTTA: I couldn't have felt any worse then how I already felt. So alone, and abandoned by you.

ANDRÉS: It was only four weeks old, right?

CARLOTTA: Almost four weeks. I didn't want that child to arrive to an empty, unhappy home.

ANDRÉS: We were too young, I didn't know what having a wife meant, much less having a child.

CARLOTTA: *(Choking up)* We were too irresponsible, we didn't deserve that child.

ANDRÉS: Is it true that it was a miscarriage?

(CARLOTTA *pours herself more wine, drinks, looks away.*)

CARLOTTA: I didn't want to be selfish, by bringing a child into this unjust world, with us so unprepared.

ANDRÉS: It would have saved us.

CARLOTTA: That's not fair on the child.

ANDRÉS: What about me? What about what you took away from me? For the first time I began to understand my relationship with my own parents, appreciating more what they had done for me. I remember myself making secret plans, for our future.

CARLOTTA: Bit you never told me any of this.

ANDRÉS: You don't regret it?

(CARLOTTA *breaks down.*)

CARLOTTA: Not one day goes by, I'm not thinking of the possibility of that child.

ANDRÉS: Thank you for telling me the truth.

CARLOTTA: I'm sorry that I lied to you.

(*Beat.* ANDRÉS *holds* CARLOTTA*'s hand.*)

ANDRÉS: I knew it. Loving a woman is a complicated thing. First you like her, then all of a sudden you're in love, and then she's roped you in, and what a burden except for the opportunity to receive the best gift a man can ever have, a woman giving you a child…my God!

(*Pause*)

CARLOTTA: I never thought of it that way. Well no wonder…

ANDRÉS: Did I tell you the story of the good Samaritan priest who fathered twenty-seven children? In the town of Cuenca, near Madrid. This compassionate man took on the humble responsibility of becoming a "love machine" to all those horny widows running around town.

CARLOTTA: Why would he do that?

ANDRÉS: Loneliness.

CARLOTTA: He should have left the priesthood.

(ANDRÉS *goes to the vegetables, and places them into the blender.*)

ANDRÉS: Not him, the women.

CARLOTTA: And then you cheated on me.

ANDRÉS: That wasn't cheating, I told you the truth, and for that you punished me.

CARLOTTA: How did you expect me to react?

ANDRÉS: Jealous, possessive and ready to do what ever it takes for your man.

CARLOTTA: *(Laughs)* We never really knew each other, did we? *(She helps set the table and serve.)*

ANDRÉS: I was also hoping it would make things a touch more exciting.

CARLOTTA: How benevolent, you were doing me a favor, like that priest.

ANDRÉS: It was stupid of me, I know. I only hurt myself in the end.

(ANDRÉS *serves the gazpacho. Sprinkles the diced vegetable garnishes on top. They sit down to eat.*)

ANDRÉS: How is it?

CARLOTTA: Very good.

(ANDRÉS *and* CARLOTTA *eat.*)

ANDRÉS: When we separated, I understood what you meant by depression.

CARLOTTA: Not pretty right?

ANDRÉS: When I left, you suffered a lot?

CARLOTTA: What do you think?

ANDRÉS: On a scale from one to ten.

CARLOTTA: What?

(ANDRÉS *opens a new cheese and cuts thin slices onto a plate.*)

ANDRÉS: I just want to get an idea of how much…

CARLOTTA: Believe me, enough.

ANDRÉS: For how long?

CARLOTTA: Long enough!

ANDRÉS: You really loved me?

CARLOTTA: I'm not answering that.

(CARLOTTA *eats.* ANDRÉS *cuts cheese.*)

ANDRÉS: And you still do.

CARLOTTA: What makes you think that?

ANDRÉS: You're here. Cheese?

(ANDRÉS *offers* CARLOTTA *a slice. She takes it.*)

ANDRÉS: *Poc, un queso de cabra.*

CARLOTTA: I love goat cheese.

ANDRÉS: I was so filled with vengeance, anger, wanting to hurt you.

CARLOTTA: Feel better?

ANDRÉS: Yes. Looking at myself in the mirror and recognizing my faults has been humbling. I used to make excuses for taking you for granted thinking it was something every man would do.

(ANDRÉS *cuts thin slices of jamón, while* CARLOTTA *pours herself more wine.*)

ANDRÉS: A little more jamón? This is Pata Negra. The best ham in the world. These black pigs roam free all day, eating only acorns.

CARLOTTA: I begged you that we see a therapist. But you'd answer, "I'd rather see a fortune teller."

(ANDRÉS *lights a cigarette.*)

ANDRÉS: I didn't even know what I was looking for in a woman.

CARLOTTA: What do you mean you didn't know?

ANDRÉS: And I'm still torn

CARLOTTA: Torn? Between?

ANDRÉS: Between the whore and the virgin.

(ANDRÉS *laughs and tries to kiss* CARLOTTA. *She pulls away.*)

CARLOTTA: You're so articulate but yet so emotionally immature.

ANDRÉS: Men will always be boys with a god complex.

CARLOTTA: Good thing there's still women left.

ANDRÉS: You would have been a great mother, Carlotta.

CARLOTTA: I don't know…

ANDRÉS: Just look at those hips…

(CARLOTTA *stares* ANDRÉS *down.*)

ANDRÉS: Made for procreating, *mi amor.*

CARLOTTA: I'm perfectly content procreating my talent.

ANDRÉS: Talent? You don't have talent.

CARLOTTA: I don't?

ANDRÉS: I don't think you do.

CARLOTTA: You don't think that every human being is born with an innate talent?

ANDRÉS: Of course not. Talent takes discipline and hard work. When someone who doesn't know you at all feels connected to you because of it, that's when you can say you've developed your talent.

CARLOTTA: That's exactly what Becky said she felt reading my work.

ANDRÉS: Becky! She doesn't count. *Te explico...* I'm good at what I do, even if it sounds presumptuous, it's okay because of my enormous talent.

CARLOTTA: So what you're saying is that I have enough talent to create a living, breathing, human being, but not enough of it to create art, because what? Art is more valuable than a child? I mean, that's what you are saying. I would have been a great mother. I'm flattered you think so! But I don't have the talent for creating art? You kidding me? Your priorities are backwards!

ANDRÉS: *Mi amor*, we're talking. How great is this? Finally, we're talking about us! About things that matter, things of consequence. Whic is what you were missing, right?

CARLOTTA: Actually, not right...

(Phone rings.)

CARLOTTA: Can you answer that, it might be the airport.

(ANDRÉS crosses to the wall phone.)

ANDRÉS: So long as it's not Becky. *(He answers phone.)* *Si? Un momento, se la paso. (Covers the mouthpiece) Para tí! (Back to phone) Encontraron la maleta? ...Aha? Aquí le paso a Carlotta Pardo.*

(CARLOTTA takes the phone.)

CARLOTTA: *Hello? ...Si entiendo, perdone...mañana? Para mañana es tarde! ...Yo no estaré aqui... Que que? ...Para la misma fecha? ...Que amables son. Claro, traiganla...*

Bueno bueno, ya está. Gracias. (She hangs up.) Por nada!
My suitcase is still in New York. They found it but it
doesn't arrive until tomorrow, at noon. They changed
our departure flight to leave out of Barcelona instead of
Madrid. How courteous of them.

ANDRÉS: You see how it was the American's fault? So
that's good, you come back in a few days.

CARLOTTA: It's okay to have the suitcase dropped off
here?

ANDRÉS: Of course. *(Pause)* You must be tired.

*(ANDRÉS tries to massage CARLOTTA's back, but she skirts
away.)*

CARLOTTA: Very.

ANDRÉS: Don't forget you have clothes here that you
might want to wear for Avila.

CARLOTTA: Oh that's right.

ANDRÉS: That polka-dot dress I love so much is still
hanging in my closet.

(CARLOTTA makes herself comfortable on the couch.)

ANDRÉS: Come lets get some sleep.

*(ANDRÉS extends his hand to CARLOTTA. She doesn't take
it.)*

CARLOTTA: I'm not sleeping with you.

ANDRÉS: Fine, then I'll sleep on the couch.

CARLOTTA: No Andy, I'm good here.

*(ANDRÉS sits down next to CARLOTTA and takes her
hands.)*

ANDRÉS: I'm glad we talked, it felt good to open up
to you, but still I'm afraid of having said the wrong
things, of not being the man you want me to be. Of
seeming selfish and crude. But we have each other

to feel comfortable and work things out. Give me a chance.

CARLOTTA: We've had enough chances.

ANDRÉS: I need to make love to you. Now, us, familiar. You must need it too. How about it, a nice, big huge orgasm to send you on your way.

CARLOTTA: You're ridiculous.

(ANDRÉS *starts to tickle* CARLOTTA, *force himself on her, playfully.*)

ANDRÉS: I know. But you don't realize just how much good that will do you.

(ANDRÉS *goes for* CARLOTTA'*s breast. She pushes his hand away.*)

CARLOTTA: Please don't do me any favors.

ANDRÉS: Who else if not your husband?

CARLOTTA: Andy, stop it.

(ANDRÉS *playfully cozies up to* CARLOTTA, *begins to caress her hair, her shoulders.*)

ANDRÉS: Okay then, let's just hug in our bed, together, like we've done so many times before.

CARLOTTA: But we need to resolve things, Andy, not keep on procrastinating.

(ANDRÉS *is practically on top of* CARLOTTA.)

ANDRÉS: Okay then, when you get back, if the divorce is what you want, I'll sign the papers and we'll celebrate with a bottle of Champagne.

CARLOTTA: You promise?

(ANDRÉS *picks* CARLOTTA *up to carry her off to the bedroom. She does not resist.*)

ANDRÉS: Yeah, yeah. I wanna make you happy, because that's the kind of man I am.

(Lights fade. When they come back up. It is six days later. Yusuf Islam's "Raihan—Thank You Allah" plays. ANDRÉS enters from bedroom, dancing to the music. He is disheveled, wearing overalls. His hands are covered in paint. He holds a paintbrush and a bucket, as he proudly studies the completed canvas that hangs on a large easel with wheels. The audience doesn't see it yet. On the table are: filled ashtrays, newspapers, a large bowl with fruit, and paper sketches for his painting, paper towels, artist materials, coffee cup, an empty wine bottle, small sculptures, including the sculpture that CARLOTTA picked up and looked at earlier. Her suitcase stands to the side.)

(The doorbell rings. ANDRÉS turns the music off, wheels the large painting to face the wall, turns off the painting spotlight and opens the door. It's CARLOTTA. She's wearing a polka-dot dress.)

ANDRÉS: *Cariño!*

(CARLOTTA sees the suitcase. ANDRÉS excitedly tries to hug her.)

CARLOTTA: Hey Andy. My suitcase. So great to see it.

(ANDRÉS looks past CARLOTTA.)

ANDRÉS: Where's Becky?

CARLOTTA: We went to see the Jewish Quarter. She'll be here in a bit.

ANDRÉS: How was Avila?

CARLOTTA: Life changing. *(She goes to her suitcase.)* The town is small but it seemed we walked for miles, going from monastery to cathedral, to convent… *(She opens her suitcase and removes a folder.)*

ANDRÉS: *Estás muy bien.* Love that dress on you. You look reinvigorated. Can we talk for a bit before you start taking things out?

CARLOTTA: Just getting the papers.

(CARLOTTA *hands the folder to* ANDRÉS, *who puts it on the table.*)

ANDRÉS: Tell me about your trip.

CARLOTTA: I told you, it was spectacular.

ANDRÉS: *Que bien*, and Becky?

CARLOTTA: What about her?

ANDRÉS: She didn't get in your way?

CARLOTTA: No. Why would she?

ANDRÉS: Can't picture her sitting still for too long.

CARLOTTA: You don't know her.

ANDRÉS: Nor do I care to.

(ANDRÉS *blocks* CARLOTTA *from the folder.*)

ANDRÉS: So go on…

CARLOTTA: About what?

ANDRÉS: Your trip, Carlotta.

CARLOTTA: Well, our first visit was to the convent where Teresa took her vows when she was barely twenty. The place is austere, cold and damp. Her room looks just like a cell; all white, unadorned, except for a cross that hangs over her tiny wooden bed, and a candle holder on her night table. Her pillow is a square, thick, dark chunk of wood. She sat to write on the cold floor by the light of a small window. No desk, no chair, no heat. She hand-wrote volumes of manuscripts filled with impeccable, flawless words. We saw her books. They're kept open, inside glass cases. Her writing expresses her inner-most thoughts about agony, doubt, love, humility, forgiveness, rapture, reptiles…

ANDRÉS: Reptiles?

CARLOTTA: She calls reptiles those inner demons we all battle with...

ANDRÉS: Do you want something to drink?

CARLOTTA: Water. You know, our fears and desires...

(ANDRÉS *takes out Vichy water from the fridge and pours two glasses.*)

ANDRÉS: *Hay vino.*

CARLOTTA: *No gracias,* water.

ANDRÉS: Take your shoes off, get comfortable, honey.

CARLOTTA: Fears and desires are the reptiles inside us.

(ANDRÉS *kisses* CARLOTTA *on the forehead and begins to massage her neck. She winces and steps back.*)

ANDRÉS: You hungry?

CARLOTTA: No thanks.

ANDRÉS: Pasa algo?

CARLOTTA: Sit down.

ANDRÉS: What is it?

(ANDRÉS *sits,* CARLOTTA *paces.*)

CARLOTTA: Inside another glass case is her finger, still wearing an emerald ring. Her body never decomposed! Supposedly, a year after she was buried, the nuns kept smelling this bouquet aroma emanating from her tomb inside the wall. So they opened it, and found that the wood of the coffin had rotted, and her clothes were torn and moldy. But her body was intact. So they bathed her, dressed her and presented her to a priest, who decided he'd cut one of her hands off, her left hand, and cut for himself a finger to carry around his neck until the day he died. That's the finger inside the display.

ANDRÉS: *Que?*

CARLOTTA: *Si.* And years later that same priest again visited Teresa's coffin, and again chopped off some more. Her heart had been pierced by an angel's arrow one day while she prayed at the altar. Now, it's inside a glass jar, with the hole still visible. Teresa wrote about that phenomenon as excruciatingly painful, yet the most pleasurable sensation driving her to moan in rapturous ecstasy.

ANDRÉS: Nice. *(Pause)* Go on.

CARLOTTA: That's all. *(Beat)* I think that priest visited Teresa's body one last time, because I hear that pieces of her are dispersed throughout churches in Europe, as relics for veneration.

ANDRÉS: *No me jodas!* I remember hearing how Franco carried a saint's arm with him everywhere he went, and when he was dying, kept it by his death bed.

CARLOTTA: It was Teresa's. Wasn't Franco like an Inquisitor?

ANDRÉS: That's what he was for Lorca, and many other innocent Spaniards.

CARLOTTA: Lorca. I need to read more of his work.

ANDRÉS: *Mira. (He searches in the bookshelf.)* Here is a good one for you.

(ANDRÉS reaches out to CARLOTTA with the book.)

CARLOTTA: No Andy. You sure?

ANDRÉS: Sure.

CARLOTTA: Thanks.

(CARLOTTA flips through the pages, lost in her thoughts. ANDRÉS sits next to her, she gets up.)

CARLOTTA: He was gay, right?

ANDRÉS: Yeah, that's why Franco had him killed. They say that before he was shot, the verbal abuse and homophobic insults were horrific. While Franco lived, Lorca's books were completely censored. *(Beat)* This compilation came out a few years ago. You'll like it.

(CARLOTTA sees BECKY kneeling to the side, in a white flowing dress. ANDRÉS does not see this.)

(Light gradually focuses on CARLOTTA as we see a projection of an abstract Virgin Mary looking down, between the columns of an immense cathedral. The rest of the room is in half-light.)

CARLOTTA: We were inside the Cathedral, when I was standing next to a huge beam of stone facing a statue of the Virgin Mary and her child…I suddenly felt a force of energy travel through me and a strong presence become apparent. I turned to my right and there before me stood a little girl in a yellow dress with a familiar face, staring right at me.

(Projection morphs into a moving one of the little girl as described.)

CARLOTTA: She was me. Her vision immediately transported me to a moment in time when that child, I stood all alone. I remembered that pretty dress, her bare legs, matching socks, shiny white shoes, and pigtails, and again felt the shock, and shame of that dreadful moment. My heart filled with an overwhelming pain, but she smiled at me and said, "everything is going to be alright". Then she walked over to Becky and kissed her on the forehead. I felt that kiss on my lips. When I looked again, she was vanishing with a wave of her hand, I felt set free. Only a minute had bone by, but to me it felt like an eternity.

(BECKY and the projection vanish. Normal light returns.)

ANDRÉS: *Mi niña,* I too had a kind of epiphany…about us…

CARLOTTA: Andy, what happened the other night was a mistake.

ANDRÉS: A mistake?

CARLOTTA: Yes, a mistake.

ANDRÉS: But it meant everything to me.

CARLOTTA: No. This time it's really over.

ANDRÉS: Okay, but that doesn't make it a mistake.

CARLOTTA: Yes. I've realized…

ANDRÉS: What?

CARLOTTA: We're in love.

ANDRÉS: Yes, we're in love.

CARLOTTA: No. Not we. Becky and…

ANDRÉS: Are you crazy?

CARLOTTA: Maybe…

ANDRÉS: Oh, *mi amor,* don't make me laugh!

CARLOTTA: I know, right?

ANDRÉS: You're kidding.

CARLOTTA: No. I'm not kidding.

ANDRÉS: You realized this while you were praying?

CARLOTTA: Yes. Praying.

ANDRÉS: You just had a little fun, and good for you… come, I want to show you something.

CARLOTTA: Love hurts you know? Love is truthful.

ANDRÉS: Look at what I've been painting since you left. You won't believe it, I saw you perfectly as the virgin queen, never before did I see you like that. *(He points to canvas.)* My truth. Come look…

(ANDRÉS tries to walk CARLOTTA over to the canvas, taking her arm, she resists.)

CARLOTTA: No. Why should I? *(She starts to wheel her suitcase.)*

ANDRÉS: Please.

CARLOTTA: You're not interested in me, I'm no virgin queen.

ANDRÉS: I think you are.

CARLOTTA: Be a friend at least.

(Buzzer sounds. ANDRÉS ignores it. It rings again.)

CARLOTTA: The door! Open your door.

ANDRÉS: No.

CARLOTTA: Why not?

(Buzzer sounds again.)

ANDRÉS: I don't want her in here.

(CARLOTTA rushes to the buzzer and presses it. Then she opens the front door.)

ANDRÉS: She should go back to where she came from, and you should stay with me, where you belong.

CARLOTTA: You've decided now that this is where I belong.

(BECKY walks in. She sees folder on table.)

ANDRÉS: It's not too late…

BECKY: Hello.

CARLOTTA: It is…

BECKY: Am I interrupting…

ANDRÉS: Yes you're interrupting

BECKY: I can come back…

CARLOTTA: No, please stay.

ANDRÉS: Becky, the innocent bystander. Coy and religious. How was the Synagogue?

BECKY: Impressive, the renovation is…

ANDRÉS: What a sight for you ha?

BECKY: Beautiful.

ANDRÉS: Makes you proud?

BECKY: Yes, a part of me is from here. My mother told me how we we're direct descendants of Nachmanides.

ANDRÉS: Nachmanides?

BECKY: Nachmanides. He was a Catalán Rabbi, doctor, philosopher, and like Saint Teresa, a mystic too.

ANDRÉS: Yeah, yeah, yeah..

BECKY: Well, according to Nachmanides, Kabbalah is the ultimate mystic truth. His books also defend man's sexual instincts as the perfect essence of nature, and His Majesty's divine intent…

ANDRÉS: His Majesty's? What's that?

BECKY: It's God. Saint Teresa calls God, his Majesty.

ANDRÉS: Great so lets undress, jump in bed and manifest "divine acts of fornication" in the name of "His Majesty". You girls seem to be following your animal instincts very organically. Or we can start with me watching from the sidelines. I'm flexible.

CARLOTTA: Oh no you're not.

ANDRÉS: Test me! I want to see what is it she can do that I can't do better.

BECKY: Love her.

ANDRÉS: *(To* BECKY*)* She's my wife.

BECKY: Really?

CARLOTTA: Just on paper.

BECKY: All the time I've known Carla, she's been alone.

ANDRÉS: Married to me!

BECKY: That she's your wife is simply a technicality.

ANDRÉS: You broke commandment number ten!

BECKY: What?

ANDRÉS: Don't covet your neighbor's wife. Don't lust after, desire, or take away your neighbor's wife!

CARLOTTA: You're quoting religion?

BECKY: Marriage involves two people, Andy.

ANDRÉS: Of the opposite sex! Don't talk to me about marriage, dyke.

(CARLOTTA *slaps* ANDRÉS.)

CARLOTTA: How dare you? Lets get out of here, Beck.

(CARLOTTA *takes* BECKY'*s arm and they begin to head out.*)

ANDRÉS: I've been married to you for thirteen years! We vowed before the altar, in a church, "Till death do us part."

CARLOTTA: Yeah, that's right, and then you left!

ANDRÉS: But I'm here, you see me, I'm always here.

CARLOTTA: Good for you.

ANDRÉS: So hold on. You've been straight all your life, I can attest to that, until that pleasurable night before... (*At* BECKY) Avila. Just a week ago. (*Back to* CARLOTTA) And now you come back a lesbian? I don't think so.

BECKY: Not uncommon...

ANDRÉS: Completely abnormal.

BECKY: If it wasn't because I understand the array of emotions you must be going through right now, I'd knock the shit right out of your stupid brain.

ANDRÉS: You're making me laugh and Saint Teresa turn in her grave.

BECKY: Why are you using religion to state your case after having so eloquently criticized it.

ANDRÉS: Yes! I am!

CARLOTTA: How convenient.

ANDRÉS: She's evil. Coaxing you with her spells. Wake up before you go to hell.

CARLOTTA: I'm awake. I'm not hurting anymore. You never loved me…

ANDRÉS: But I know you, and you're not a lesbian, Carlotta.

CARLOTTA: And what if I am?

ANDRÉS: You're life will be chaos.

BECKY: "Chaos is the expression of the divine out of which all things are created."

ANDRÉS: Shut up! In my country we don't butt in where we're not invited.

BECKY: From where I come, not being invited doesn't stop us.

ANDRÉS: And you're proud of that?

BECKY: If that's what it takes. I love her.

(ANDRÉS *flings the sculpture off the table.*)

CARLOTTA: Andy don't! (*She runs to pick up the pieces.*) It's your work, don't do that. (*She places all the pieces on the table trying to put them together, and when she sees that there is one missing, she gets back on the floor looking for it, desperate, crying.*) A piece is missing.

(BECKY *starts to look as well.*)

ANDRÉS: Where do I sign?

BECKY: Here it is. (*She sets it on the table next to the other pieces.*)

CARLOTTA: You wanna sign?

ANDRÉS: No, but that's why you came here. *(He opens the file and waves the papers.)*

CARLOTTA: That's not really why...

ANDRÉS: Lets get this done with, once and for all!

CARLOTTA: Okay. *(She takes the papers and points where he needs to sign.)* "Irreconcilable differences." *Que mierda es esa?*

CARLOTTA: *Incompatibididad de caracteres.* Sign here, and the other three red marks.

(ANDRÉS signs.)

ANDRÉS: By the way, you two can now get married in New York.

(CARLOTTA takes the signed papers.)

CARLOTTA: I'll send you a copy when it's stamped by the court.

ANDRÉS: Don't forget it. I want to see what conceptual artwork comes out of it.

(ANDRÉS crosses to the kitchen. BECKY and CARLOTTA start to leave.)

CARLOTTA: Bye.

ANDRÉS: You promised we'd have a glass of champagne afterwards.

(BECKY and CARLOTTA look at each other.)

BECKY: *(Touched)* That's fine.

ANDRÉS: I'm sorry, was I talking to you?

(ANDRÉS pops open the bottle, and fills three glasses. While CARLOTTA sneaks a kiss on BECKY's lips.)

CARLOTTA: *(Mouthing)* I love you.

BECKY: *(Reassured)* I love you.

(BECKY and CARLOTTA smile into each other's eyes.)

ANDRÉS: I gotta say, I never expected this.

(ANDRÉS *hands the glasses to* BECKY *and* CARLOTTA.)

CARLOTTA: I didn't either.

ANDRÉS: *(Raising his glass)* To the mastermind of it all.

BECKY: *(Raising her glass)* To Teresa, who insists that we don't retreat from the unfamiliar, if it's our heart's intent, because that supersedes church law, authority, and anything oppressive.

(BECKY *and* CARLOTTA *drink.*)

CARLOTTA: *(Raising her glass) Salud.*

ANDRÉS: Why? Why with someone of your own sex?

BECKY: And deny myself the all powerful penis?

ANDRÉS: It's just not natural.

BECKY: But women are more beautiful, interesting, nurturing, giving…

ANDRÉS: Yeah, and they can also be more impertinent, sly and devious.

BECKY: That too.

(CARLOTTA *hands* ANDRÉS *the glasses.* BECKY *walks over to the painting.*)

CARLOTTA: We tried, Andy.

BECKY: Wow!

ANDRÉS: I should have signed those papers when you mailed them to me the first time.

BECKY: This is really beautiful…

ANDRÉS: *Es una mierda!*

BECKY: It's brilliant.

ANDRÉS: My only pleasure will be destroying it.

BECKY: Please don't.

ANDRÉS: Don't you tell me what to do.

BECKY: I'm not…

ANDRÉS: It's shit!

BECKY: I'll take it.

ANDRÉS: Oh, you want to take my art too, huh? Anything else Miss Becky? You cut off my balls, you take my wife and now you want to take away my pleasure destroying it?

BECKY: No, no, not like that, I meant…

ANDRÉS: Just get out. Just get the fuck out!

CARLOTTA: We're going.

(BECKY *takes her suitcase.*)

BECKY: I was complimenting your talent, that's all.

ANDRÉS: Spare me.

BECKY: Meet you outside. *(She exits.)*

(CARLOTTA *stops to look at the canvas.*)

CARLOTTA: …You got me. You really got me. *(Steps toward* ANDRÉS.*)*

ANDRÉS: Go.

(CARLOTTA *retreats.*)

CARLOTTA: I'm sorry that that's not me anymore.

(As the lights begin to fade, CARLOTTA *turns to take one last look at the painting. Then she exits.)*

*(*ANDRÉS *goes to the C D player and plays* A Wild World.*)*

(An ethereal light slowly and subtly illuminates the painting as ANDRÉS *takes a can of black paint and a thick brush. He goes to the painting and without looking at it, lifts the black paint-filled brush. He lets the paint drip to the ground. He drops the brush and falls to his knees, almost as if he were*

praying before his painting, as the lights fade, illuminating
only his painting of CARLOTTA. *Then: blackout.)*

END OF PLAY